Food

La comida

lah koh-*mee*-dah

Illustrated by Clare Beaton

Ilustraciones de Clare Beaton

bread

el pan

ehl pahn

fruits

las frutas

lahs *froo*-tahs

egg

el huevo

ehl *weh*-voh

cheese

el queso

ehl *keh*-soh

ice cream

el helado

ehl eh-*lah*-doh

fruit juice

el jugo de fruta

ehl *hoo*-goh deh *froo*-tah

cake

el pastel

ehl pahs-tell

chicken

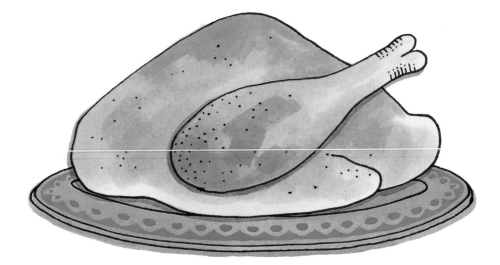

el pollo

ehl *poh*-yoh

cookie

la galleta

lah gah-*yeh*-tah

ham

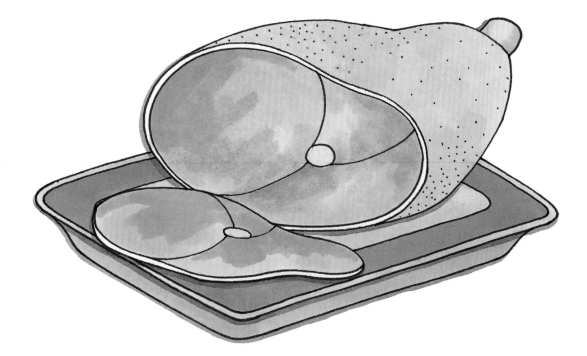

el jamón

ehl hah-*mohn*

milk

la leche

lah *leh*-cheh

A simple guide to pronouncing the Spanish words★

- Read this guide as naturally as possible, as if it were English.
- Put stress on the letters in *italics*, e.g. ehl *keh*-soh.

la comida	lah koh-*mee*-dah	**food**
el pan	ehl pahn	**bread**
las frutas	lahs *froo*-tahs	**fruits**
el huevo	ehl *weh*-voh	**egg**
el queso	ehl *keh*-soh	**cheese**
el helado	ehl eh-*lah*-doh	**ice cream**
el jugo de fruta	ehl *hoo*-goh deh *froo*-tah	**fruit juice**
el pastel	ehl pahs-*tell*	**cake**
el pollo	ehl *poh*-yoh	**chicken**
la galleta	lah gah-*yeh*-tah	**cookie**
el jamón	ehl hah-*mohn*	**ham**
la leche	lah *leh*-cheh	**milk**

★There are many different guides to pronunciation. Our guide attempts to balance precision with simplicity.

11-18-04   13·49
Text and illustrations © Copyright 2003 by B SMALL PUBLISHING, Surrey, England.
First edition for the United States, its Dependencies, Canada, and the Philippines published in 2003 by Barron's Educational Series, Inc.
Address all inquiries to:
Barron's Educational Series, Inc., 250 Wireless Boulevard, Hauppauge, New York 11788. (*http://www.barronseduc.com*)
International Standard Book Number 0-7641-2609-1
Library of Congress Control Number 2003101095
Printed in Hong Kong   9 8 7 6 5 4 3 2 1